You Don't Look 35,
Charlie Brown!

You Don't Look 35, Charlie Brown!

Charles M. Schulz

HOLT, RINEHART AND WINSTON   NEW YORK

Copyright © 1985 by United Feature Syndicate, Inc.
Based on the PEANUTS® comic strip by Charles M. Schulz
All rights reserved, including the right to reproduce this
book or portions thereof in any form.
Published by Holt, Rinehart and Winston,
383 Madison Avenue, New York, New York 10017.
Published simultaneously in Canada by Holt, Rinehart and
Winston of Canada, Limited.

Library of Congress Catalog Card Number: 85-81217
ISBN Hardcover: 0-03-005859-7
ISBN Paperback: 0-03-005624-1

First Edition
Printed in the United States of America
1 3 5 7 9 10 8 6 4 2

ISBN 0-03-005859-7 HARDBOUND

ISBN 0-03-005624-1 PAPERBACK

A cartoonist is someone who has to draw the same thing day after day after day without repeating himself.

I probably spend more time than is good for me either reliving or regretting the past, but that kind of thinking is partly what cartoons are made of. For my thirty-fifth anniversary book, I wanted to write something a little bit different, so here are a few thoughts and recollections that have inspired, either directly or indirectly, some comic strips and Sunday pages. This is not the answer to the much asked question of where ideas come from, for I really can't answer that, but it does suggest how some of the prompting comes about.

Charles M. Schulz

My earliest recollection of drawing and getting credit for it and being complimented on it is from kindergarten. I think it was my first day, and the teacher gave us huge sheets of white paper, large black crayons, and told us to draw anything we wanted. I drew a man shoveling snow, and she came around, paused, looked at my picture, and said, "Someday, Charles, you're going to be an artist." Now she wasn't quite right— she didn't say "cartoonist"—but there was an interesting aspect to this. I had drawn the snow shovel as a square, but I knew this was not right. I knew nothing about perspective, and didn't know how to fix it, but I knew that something wasn't right about this picture. I like to think there was some anticipation there of what was to come.

When I was in the first grade, the teacher put a valentine box on a table in front of the room. It was two days before Valentine's Day and we were to bring to school the cards we wanted to give to the kids we liked. Obviously, there were some I liked more than others, but because I didn't wish to offend anyone, I made out a list that included everyone. My mother helped me select all the cards, and I took them to school the next day. Classrooms are pretty big to a first grader, and it was a long walk from where I sat up to the front of the room where the valentine box waited. Everyone could watch you as you walked to the front of the room and dropped each card through the slit on top of the box.

I couldn't do it. I took all the valentines home.

CHARLIE BROWN, I'VE BEEN FEELING AWFULLY GUILTY ABOUT NOT GIVING YOU A VALENTINE THIS YEAR...I'D LIKE FOR YOU TO HAVE THIS ONE

HOLD ON THERE! WHAT DO YOU THINK YOU'RE DOING? WHO DO YOU THINK YOU ARE?!

WHERE WERE YOU FEBRUARY 14th WHEN EVERYONE ELSE WAS GIVING OUT VALENTINES? IS KINDNESS AND THOUGHTFULNESS SOMETHING YOU CAN MAKE RETROACTIVE? DON'T YOU THINK HE HAS ANY FEELINGS?!

YOU AND YOUR FRIENDS ARE THE MOST THOUGHTLESS BUNCH I'VE EVER KNOWN! YOU DON'T CARE ANYTHING ABOUT CHARLIE BROWN! YOU JUST HATE TO FEEL GUILTY!

AND NOW YOU HAVE THE NERVE TO COME AROUND A WHOLE MONTH LATER, AND OFFER HIM A USED VALENTINE JUST TO EASE YOUR CONSCIENCE! WELL, LET ME TELL YOU SOMETHING... CHARLIE BROWN DOESN'T NEED YOUR...

DON'T INTERFERE... **I'LL TAKE IT!**

The living rooms in the homes of our friends when we were little varied a good deal. They looked different and they smelled different. Some we were allowed to play in. Others we only walked through. Some we never saw at all. If the home contained an older sister, we never talked to her. Older sisters were awesome.

Panel 1: HAVE YOU EVER NOTICED HOW CERTAIN HOMES HAVE DISTINCT COOKING ODORS?

Panel 2: YOU MEAN LIKE GARLIC OR SPAGHETTI?

Panel 3: I KNOW ONE KID'S HOUSE THAT ALWAYS SMELLS LIKE THEY'VE BEEN COOKING CABBAGE

Panel 4: OURS SMELLS LIKE TV DINNERS!

Panel 1: CHARLIE BROWN SAYS THAT BROTHERS AND SISTERS CAN LEARN TO GET ALONG...

Panel 2: HE SAYS THEY CAN GET ALONG THE SAME WAY MATURE ADULTS GET ALONG...

Panel 3: AND HE SAYS THAT ADULTS CAN GET ALONG THE SAME WAY THAT NATIONS GET ALONG...

Panel 4: AT THIS POINT THE ANALOGY BREAKS DOWN!

MADAM FULLCHARGE

Panel 1: YOU DON'T THINK MY BROTHER AND I GET ALONG VERY WELL, DO YOU?

Panel 2: YOU JUST WAIT....SOMEDAY, AFTER WE'RE GROWN, WE'LL BE VERY CLOSE!

Panel 3: WHAT DOES SHE MEAN BY "CLOSE"?

Panel 4: WE MAY BOTH LIVE ON THE SAME CONTINENT!

I ALMOST BOUGHT YOU A BIRTHDAY PRESENT JUST NOW

I SAW THIS BOTTLE OF COLOGNE IN A STORE WINDOW, AND IT ONLY COST A DOLLAR...

I KNEW IT WOULD MAKE YOU HAPPY TO GET IT, BUT THEN I SAW SOMETHING THAT I KNEW WOULD MAKE YOU EVEN MORE HAPPY!

IN THE WINDOW OF THE STORE NEXT DOOR, THERE WAS A SALAMI SANDWICH WHICH ALSO COST A DOLLAR...NOW, I KNOW HOW CONCERNED YOU ARE FOR THE PEOPLES OF THIS WORLD...

I KNOW HOW HAPPY IT'S GOING TO MAKE YOU WHEN I BECOME A FAMOUS DOCTOR, AND CAN HELP THE PEOPLE OF THE WORLD

BUT IF I'M GOING TO BECOME A DOCTOR, I'M GOING TO HAVE TO GET GOOD GRADES IN SCHOOL...

AND TO GET GOOD GRADES, I'M GOING TO HAVE TO STUDY, AND IN ORDER TO STUDY, I HAVE TO BE HEALTHY...

IN ORDER TO BE HEALTHY, I HAVE TO EAT...SO INSTEAD OF THE COLOGNE, I BOUGHT THE SANDWICH...ALL FOR YOUR HAPPINESS!

I'M SO HAPPY I COULD CRY!

When I was in the sixth grade, there would frequently be interruptions in our class as a particular boy was suddenly ordered to go to the principal's office. Soon he would return with a nice grin on his face, wearing a striking leather belt with an attached shoulder strap and a silver badge. Everyone in the class would applaud, for it meant that he had been chosen to be on the school patrol. I never achieved this honor, probably because I was not considered forceful enough, and was also either the smallest or the next-to-the-smallest kid in class. I did get to be substitute, however, but that never rated the leather Sam Browne belt. Girls were never chosen. Somehow, not being chosen bothered me only a little. I simply decided that I was not quite good enough, and let it go at that. It would have been nice, though, to have walked into the class with that leather belt.

MARCIE, I DON'T NEED YOU TO HELP ME ACROSS THE STREET!

RULES ARE RULES! I'M THE PATROL PERSON, AND I'LL TELL YOU WHEN YOU CAN GO ACROSS!

ALL RIGHT, EVERYBODY, LET'S GO! QUICKLY NOW! TO THE OTHER SIDE! QUICKLY NOW! QUICKLY!

IT'S ONLY THREE O'CLOCK, BUT AS SOON AS I GET HOME, I'M GOING TO BED!

WHY SHOULD MARCIE GET TO BE A PATROL PERSON AND NOT ME?

I CAN'T STAND IT!

THIS IS NOT LIKE ME..

I'M INTO JEALOUSY, CHUCK!

YOU LOOK TIRED, MARCIE

I AM, SIR.. I GOT UP AT SIX O'CLOCK SO I COULD BE AT MY PATROL POST ON TIME

I'M SO SLEEPY... I DON'T THINK I CAN STAY AWAKE MUCH...

...LONGER..
Z

I used to own the very first copy of *Famous Funnies* that was ever published. I don't have the slightest idea what happened to it. Other comic magazines began to imitate *Famous Funnies*, and I bought every one that came out. One of the stores lost me as a customer, however, when the man behind the counter said to me once too often, "Going to do some heavy reading, eh?"

THIS IS WHAT I ENJOY.. A MID-AFTERNOON SNACK...

I THINK I LIKE CEREAL MORE IN THE AFTERNOON THAN I DO IN THE MORNING...

NOW, I HAVE TO FIND SOMETHING TO READ WHILE I EAT MY COLD CEREAL, AND I HAVE TO FIND IT FAST BEFORE THE CEREAL GETS SOGGY...

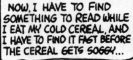

I CAN'T STAND TO EAT COLD CEREAL WITHOUT HAVING SOMETHING TO READ..

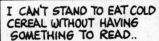

RATS! SOMEBODY TOOK THE SPORTS SECTION OUT OF THE MORNING PAPER! AND WHERE'S THE FUNNIES? THEY TOOK THE FUNNIES, TOO! GOOD GRIEF!

"MOBY DICK"...NO, I DON'T WANT TO START THAT RIGHT NOW..."THE INTERPRETER'S BIBLE"....TWELVE VOLUMES...THAT'S A LITTLE TOO MUCH FOR ONE BOWL OF CEREAL.."BLEAK HOUSE"...NO..."JOSEPH ANDREWS"...NO..

THIS IS TERRIBLE! I'VE GOT TO FIND SOMETHING FAST!

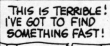

COMIC MAGAZINES! HAVE I READ ALL OF THEM?

I'VE READ THAT ONE, AND THAT ONE, AND THIS ONE, AND THAT ONE, AND THIS ONE, AND THIS ONE, AND...

I HAVEN'T READ THIS ONE!

SOGGY!

Schulz

I can't remember if I was in the eighth or ninth grade, but I do know that in one of those art classes I learned the most important lesson of my life about creativity. Each year when one of the professional ice shows came to St. Paul, art students were given a chance to compete for free tickets by creating posters advertising the shows. I drew a very good Popeye those days and could letter quite well. The other kids in class mostly drew either a man or a woman skating. My poster showed Popeye skating and my poster lettering was, in my mind, much superior to all the others and, especially, that of Stanley, the young fellow who sat next to me and who had drawn, of all things, a polar bear coming out of an igloo. What in the world did that have to do with an ice show?

"Your poster is really neat, Charles," the kids would say to me. "You're going to win for sure." I didn't, of course, for the judges saw something original in Stanley's polar bear compared to all the other dull skating figures and copied Popeyes. It was a good lesson.

WHAT'S THIS? **OH, IT'S JUST A LITTLE PICTURE I DREW OF A MAN ON A HORSE...**

OH, I JUST LOVE HORSE PICTURES!

COULD I HAVE IT, CHARLIE BROWN? COULD I HAVE IT TO HANG ON MY WALL?

WELL, I GUESS SO... IF YOU THINK IT'S GOOD ENOUGH...I MEAN.. **AND HOW ABOUT SIGNING IT? WILL YOU SIGN IT, TOO? WILL YOU PUT YOUR NAME ON IT?**

ALL RIGHT..WHAT DO YOU WANT ME TO DO...JUST SIGN MY NAME, OR... **YOU WERE GOING TO DO IT, WEREN'T YOU?**

HA!HA!HA!HA! HA!HA!HA!HA!

YOU REALLY THOUGHT I WANTED TO HANG THIS STUPID PICTURE ON MY WALL, DIDN'T YOU? HA!HA!HA!HA!

..AND HE EVEN THOUGHT I WANTED HIM TO SIGN IT! HA!HA!HA!HA! **I CAN'T STAND IT!**

SCHULZ

Most of our baseball games were pickup games with guys from other neighborhoods, although for one summer when I was fourteen we had an organized four-team league due to the arrangements of our local playground director. Unlike today's Little League, parents were virtually nonexistent as spectators, but during this same fourteen-year-old summer we began playing softball games in the evening after we had all had dinner (or as we called it in the midwest, "supper"). One of the fathers would frequently join these games, and because he was a pleasant fellow and played quite well, we always welcomed his presence and, in fact, envied the kid who had such an athletic father. Not that we were at all critical of our own fathers, for we were well aware of the difficulties of the Depression, and knew how hard they worked, but still, the envy was there. A few years later we discovered that this man's marriage was very shaky, and he was probably only too happy to get out of the house and play softball with the kids after dinner.

TWO OUTS ALREADY.. I CAN'T STAND IT!

OKAY, LUCY, WE NEED A RUN..HERE'S WHAT I WANT YOU TO DO...

IF YOU GET ON FIRST, WATCH FOR MY SIGNAL TO STEAL SECOND...I'LL TUG MY EAR LIKE THIS...

NOW, IF YOU GET TO SECOND, AND I WANT YOU TO STEAL AGAIN, I'LL CLAP MY HANDS LIKE THIS...

IF YOU GET TO THIRD, AND I WANT YOU TO STAY THERE, I'LL TUG MY OTHER EAR LIKE THIS, BUT IF I WANT YOU TO TRY TO STEAL HOME, I'LL RUB THE FRONT OF MY SHIRT...

STRIKE ONE!

STRIKE TWO!

STRIKE THREE!!

THAT WAS EASIER THAN TRYING TO REMEMBER ALL THOSE SIGNALS!

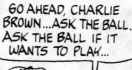

The opening day baseball game at Lexington Park in St. Paul was always cause for excitement, and for some reason those of us who wanted to attend were released from school early. I was a junior in high school at the time, and was only too willing to accept this legitimate opportunity to avoid afternoon classes. Strangely enough, not many took advantage of this break, but I still remember getting to the park early and seeing a girl from our school come down the aisle and sit near me. What intrigued me was a large notebook she opened wherein she had ruled out in pencil a complete box score preparatory to keeping track of the plays of everyone in the game. Something about the diligence of a young girl who, because she obviously could not afford to buy a real scorecard, had so carefully made her own, saddened me. I should have talked to her, but I didn't have the nerve.

The Park Theater was a movie house across the street and down about a half block from my dad's barbershop. The changing of attractions was always fascinating, even though they were regular. One feature ran on Sunday and Monday. The next ran from Tuesday through Thursday, and the next on Friday and Saturday, with a matinee and serial on that last afternoon. I always liked coming out of the theater at night after the last show and seeing one of the ushers standing on a ladder changing the letters that spelled out the next attraction. When I was eight years old, my mother took me to my first Saturday matinee. The serial was called *The Jade Box*, and I remember only two scenes; some men in an open touring car dressed in formal wear trying to escape from someone, crashing through a wooden road barrier. In the other scene, some blood seeped under the wall from one room to another.

On succeeding Saturdays we also saw Rin Tin Tin and some Bobby Jones shorts. After the latter, I asked my mother to buy me a golf club. It was a niblick, a toy, of course, with a head made out of lead. I took it onto the playground that was across the street from where we lived, and having no golf balls, began to hit small pebbles. A tiny friend lined the pebbles up for me, and all went well until he placed one in the line that was a bit too large, and the club head broke. It was another seven years before I got to play a real game of golf.

Amos and Andy were at the height of their popularity on radio. We never missed listening at nine o'clock each evening. One night in the middle of a movie, my mother and dad began discussing something, and then leaned toward me and whispered, "Which would you rather do, see the rest of the movie, or go home and listen to Amos and Andy?" We went home to the radio.

Several years later, I imagine when I was about ten, the theater advertised a free Butterfinger candy bar to the first one hundred kids attending that Saturday's matinee. I stood in line and as I approached the box office, saw the last candy bar disappear. I was the one-hundred-and-first!

When I was nine or ten, and my parents would go out someplace, my grandmother and I would go to the theater that was right around the corner. After the comedy short, and maybe one of those pieces I hated, with an orchestra playing on screen, they would have either Paramount News or Movietone News. The newsreel would always finish with "The End," and I was always afraid my grandmother would say, "Well, let's go home!" I would invariably turn to her and say, "Grandma, that just means that the news is over and the movie is about to begin," and she would always say, "Yes, I know." It took me about forty years to realize that grandma was a lot smarter than I thought she was.

Panel 1: MY GRANDMOTHER HELPED TO MAKE THIS COUNTRY GREAT!

Panel 2: DURING WORLD WAR II, SHE WORKED AS A RIVETER, AND WROTE LETTERS TO SEVENTEEN SERVICEMEN!

Panel 3: TALK ABOUT WOMEN IN HISTORY...

Panel 4: LET'S HEAR IT FOR MY GRANDMOTHER!!

Panel 1: MY GRANDMOTHER LOVED TO DANCE

Panel 2: EVERY SATURDAY NIGHT SHE AND HER FRIENDS WENT TO THIS LITTLE PLACE THAT HAD A JUKE BOX, AND A DANCE FLOOR AND SIX BOOTHS...

Panel 3: SHE WAS THE FIRST ONE TO CARVE THOSE IMMORTAL WORDS ON THE BACK OF ONE OF THE BOOTHS, "**KILROY WAS HERE**"

Panel 4: ACTUALLY, ALTHOUGH GRANDMA WAS A LOT OF FUN, SHE WASN'T VERY CREATIVE!

Panel 1: AND SO, WORLD WAR II CAME TO AN END...

Panel 2: MY GRANDMOTHER LEFT HER JOB IN THE DEFENSE PLANT, AND WENT TO WORK FOR THE TELEPHONE COMPANY...

Panel 3: WE NEED TO STUDY THE LIVES OF GREAT WOMEN LIKE MY GRANDMOTHER... TALK TO YOUR OWN GRANDMOTHER TODAY... ASK HER QUESTIONS...

Panel 4: YOU'LL FIND SHE KNOWS MORE THAN PEANUT BUTTER COOKIES! THANK YOU!

Deer

THAT SHOULD BE "DEAR"

IN THE SALUTATION OF A LETTER, THE PROPER WORD AND SPELLING OF THAT WORD IS "DEAR"

Deer are beautiful animals found in most parts of the world.

I'M SORRY... I DIDN'T REALIZE YOU WERE WRITING ABOUT DEER... I APOLOGIZE...

WELL, I SHOULD HOPE SO! IT SEEMS TO ME THAT A LOT OF THE PROBLEMS IN THIS WORLD ARE CAUSED BY PEOPLE WHO CRITICIZE OTHER PEOPLE BEFORE THEY KNOW WHAT THEY'RE TALKING ABOUT!

Dear Grandma,

I never knew either of my grandfathers and only one grandmother, Sophia Halverson, my mother's mother, who lived off and on with us most of my life. To me, she was always an old lady, although it could very well be that I am now as old as she was when she first lived with my mother, dad, and me. She was much wrinkled, had increasing hearing problems, was always dependent on her children, and suffered one of the worst tragedies that can come to a mother; she outlived six of her nine children. She loved sports, but knew almost nothing about the real details of any. When Patty Berg became prominent in the Minnesota golfing area, my grandmother always checked the papers to see if Patty had won, although she had to ask me which was the better score, a high one or a low one.

Our house had a typical Minnesota basement with an open area beneath the stairs. The space beneath the stairs and the supporting post was about six feet and made a pretty good facsimile of a hockey goal. Being very accommodating, my grandmother would take a broom that I gave her and stand in front of this make-believe goal while I shot tennis balls at her with a hockey stick. I like to think she made a lot of great saves.

Dear Grandma,
How are you? I am fine.

I have been working hard in school.

WHICH GRANDMA ARE YOU WRITING TO? WE HAVE TWO GRANDMAS, YOU KNOW...

I AM WELL AWARE OF THAT! I AM ALSO AWARE THAT THEY DON'T LIKE EACH OTHER...

AND THAT BRINGS UP A PROBLEM...

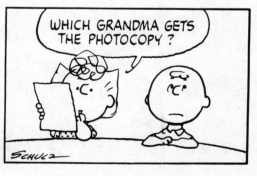

WHICH GRANDMA GETS THE PHOTOCOPY?

SCHULZ

FANTASTIC!

HAVE YOU EVER KNOWN ANYONE WHO HAS THE GIFT OF PROPHECY?

JUST MYSELF

YOU?!

ABSOLUTELY! I CAN PREDICT WHAT ANY ADULT WILL ANSWER WHEN HE OR SHE IS ASKED A CERTAIN QUESTION

IF YOU GO UP TO AN ADULT, AND SAY, "HOW COME WE HAVE A MOTHER'S DAY AND A FATHER'S DAY, BUT WE DON'T HAVE A CHILDREN'S DAY?" THAT ADULT WILL ALWAYS ANSWER, "EVERY DAY IS CHILDREN'S DAY!"

IT DOESN'T MATTER WHAT ADULT YOU ASK... YOU WILL ALWAYS GET THE SAME ANSWER...IT IS AN ABSOLUTE CERTAINTY!

I'LL TRY IT OUT ON GRANDMA...

GRANDMA, HOW COME WE HAVE A MOTHER'S DAY AND A FATHER'S DAY, BUT WE DON'T HAVE A CHILDREN'S DAY?

EVERY DAY IS CHILDREN'S DAY

THE GIFT OF PROPHECY!

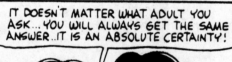

Children do not converse. They say things. They ask, they tell, and they talk, but they know nothing of one of the great joys in life, conversation. Then, along about twelve, give or take a year on either side, two young people sitting on their bicycles near a front porch on a summer evening begin to talk about others that they know, and conversation is discovered. Some confuse conversation with talking, of course, and go on for the rest of their lives, never stopping, boring others with meaningless chatter and complaints. But real conversation includes asking questions, and asking the right questions before it is too late.

In 1980 I was part of a panel that was requested to appear before four hundred exceptional high school students. Each of us on the panel was to talk for only a few minutes on any subject that we thought appropriate. Some talked of the greatness of our country; one dragged out a standard anticommunist speech, but all tried to say something that might be of use to the young people in the audience. My turn was coming up, and I still hadn't decided what useful thing a cartoonist had to contribute other than the trite recommendations of dedication and hard work. Something else had been working its way forward in my mind, however, in recent weeks, and I decided to gamble on it even though it was very personal to each listener.

"I am not one to give advice," I said, "and always hesitated to do so with my own children, but tonight I am going to give you some advice that is very important . . ." I then told them to go home and begin asking questions of their parents, to stop saying things to their parents, and instead begin asking things about their parents' pasts that demonstrate a real interest, and pursue the questioning. "Don't stop until you have learned something about your father's first job or your mother's early dreams. It will take energy, but it will be infinitely worthwhile, and it must be done now. It must be done before it is too late."

I didn't exactly get fired from a job I had working in a grocery store when I was eighteen, but I was certainly "let go." As a clerk, I was utterly hopeless. I never knew the price of anything, and never developed the skill of being really useful. I was a good delivery boy, however, and almost enjoyed filling the miserable truck that was all the owners could afford, and driving around certain areas of St. Paul delivering the groceries to homes sometimes guarded by barking dogs. One Chow dog refused ever to let me near the house. Another Irish setter got into the bag of groceries that I left on the back steps of a house where no one answered the doorbell. The grocery store was a small one on the front edge of a red brick apartment complex. One of the customers was a beautiful dark-haired housewife who was probably in her early twenties. She always answered the door in a sheer dressing gown. She also was the only one who ever gave me a tip for delivering the groceries. After paying me what she owed, she always gave me a nickel. The job ended suddenly on a Saturday afternoon when one of the women who was part owner of the store paid me my regular nine dollars and said they really didn't need me anymore. It didn't bother me a bit.

During my senior year in high school and for most of the next year, I took the lessons of the Federal Schools' correspondence course. I didn't always have the right drawing paper, and soon learned that the stiff white cardboard used by the laundry when they returned shirts was not really suitable for good pen and ink work. Actually, I learned a good deal from the correspondence course, and after "graduating" used to drive from St. Paul over to Minneapolis where the school was located, to get personal criticism from Frank Wing. His style was of the old school, and he had difficulty explaining to me why my style was still not appropriate. It is very hard to explain to a young person why the supposedly crude drawings in Popeye were actually wonderful. I tried sending in gag cartoons, but collected only form rejection slips.

One day, my mother suggested that perhaps my cartoons weren't "smutty" enough. She chose the word carefully, and I believe accurately for that day. My problem, however, was that I couldn't have drawn a "smutty" cartoon if I had tried. One day, I answered an ad for a "junior artist." It was a direct mail advertising firm in downtown Minneapolis. The boss had me fill out a questionnaire that called for a couple of simple drawings, and amazingly enough, I found myself hired as a "junior artist." Unfortunately, the title was a ruse to get a delivery boy. When I asked the lady who was in charge of getting material delivered throughout the downtown area when I was going to get to do some drawing, she said, "Oh, no, he did it again! He hires young guys as 'junior artists' when he only wants delivery boys!"

At the end of the first pay period, I took my money to a local department store and bought a cartoon collection called *Colliers Collects Its Wits*. During the lunch hour, I sat at a table looking through the book when the other young fellow who was not an artist, but actually a bona fide delivery boy, asked me what I was reading. It was beyond his comprehension. He could not understand why anyone would pay two dollars and fifty cents for a book of cartoons.

I went through two more delivery boy jobs before finally ending up at another direct mail advertising firm in downtown St. Paul, where I worked in a small room with four other young men tying bundles of tabloid-size papers together. We did this from eight until four-thirty, and for the first few days, I thought I would lose my mind. But almost all jobs have some kind of satisfaction to them, and we soon developed pride in our speed and dexterity in tying up the bundles.

Also, there were two charming girls in their early twenties, named June and Marie, who sometimes sat at a table in our room addressing labels. I found that I could laugh and joke with them, and discovered the wonderful feeling for the first time in my life of being liked.

Eventually the owners of the business found out that I could draw and do lettering. They began to let me work on mimeograph layouts drawing simple cartoons. In between these projects I also made deliveries around town. The company did well for itself. It got a cartoonist and a delivery boy for sixteen dollars a week.

The gag writer was also developing. One day just before the new year, I was assigned the task of going around the downtown area on foot to deliver the new firm calendars to all their best customers. When I left the office, the foreman told me to call back in after an hour or so to see if they needed me for anything. After working my way from building to building, I soon found myself several miles from our office with a light snow falling. I called back as ordered, and the foreman asked, "Where are you?"

"I'm not sure," I said. "All I know is I just saw a buffalo walk by!" The gag writer (or smart aleck) was on his way.

After the war, my first job was doing free-lance lettering for comic magazines where everybody else did the drawing. I lettered not only in English, but in French and Spanish too, even though I didn't know those languages. I would do them sitting in my kitchen at night after my regular job was over. Then I'd get up early, drive downtown to St. Paul, leave off the pages I had lettered, and drive to my regular job. Did I regard having to work two jobs as a hardship? No! I regarded it as something great. I was involved. I was doing something with cartoons.

Whenever I am asked about the origin of the name "Peanuts," I always manage to slip in a little dig that it is the worst name ever thought of for a comic strip. The original title was to have been "Li'l Folks," (admittedly, not much better) but "Tack" Knight, the creator of "Little Folks," a strip that was no longer running, asked us not to use our title because he thought he might someday revive his characters.

Larry Rutman of United Feature Syndicate, who was eventually to become one of my very best friends, and treated me almost like a son or nephew, or something, called me and said we needed a new title. All I could think of was "Charlie Brown," or "Good Ol' Charlie Brown." The syndicate people didn't care for those, and then informed me that they had the perfect title, "Peanuts." I was horrified, and called Larry immediately and told him it was a terrible title. It was undignified, inappropriate, and confusing. I said that readers would almost certainly think it was the name of the lead character, and that no one ever referred to small children as "peanuts."

"Well," he said, "the salesmen are ready to take the feature on the road, and we think it's a title that will catch the attention of editors." What could a young unknown from St. Paul say? I gave in. Years later, I was told by Bill Anderson, their production manager, that he had been asked to try to think of a title for a new kid strip United was about to launch so he wrote a list of ten possibilities, one of which was "Peanuts." He said he had never seen the strip.

About three years later I was visiting New York, and was taken by Larry Rutman for lunch at the weekly meeting of the Dutch Treat Club. I remember Victor Borge as being the afternoon entertainer. At one point, the regular members passed little cards up to the chairman indicating who their guests were. He looked at the cards, read off the names, and as each guest stood, made some remark. "Larry Rutman," he said, "has as his guest today Charles Schulz, the creator of 'Peanuts.' Now isn't that a hell of a thing to be the creator of?!" I turned to Larry and said, "See?"

When I began to draw the kids in the strip really talking to each other, or maybe thinking about something, the obvious pose was sitting on a curb much the way the characters in the early *Skippy* strips by Percy Crosby were drawn. Almost immediately, however, and maybe because I had children of my own, I became sensitive about showing them sitting where they could easily be hit by a car. Eventually I developed the brick or sometimes stone wall, and showed them behind it leaning on their arms staring out at the world.

One day I started to build a stone wall myself behind our driveway at home as kind of a therapeutic exercise. It was not at all beautiful and certainly had no useful purpose other than to get me out in the sun and make me feel that I was really doing something. As the wall began slowly to take shape, my wife, Jeannie, came out to look at it and remarked, "That looks just like the wall you draw in the strip!"

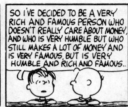

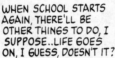

I don't know why there's so much unrequited love in my strip. I seem to be fascinated by unrequited love, if not obsessed by it: Sally loves Linus, Linus can't stand her; Lucy loves Schroeder, Schroeder can't stand her; Charlie Brown loves the red-haired girl, but doesn't even dare to go near her. There's something funny about unrequited love—I suppose it's because we can all identify with it. We've all been turned down by someone we love, and it's probably the most bitter blow in life.

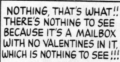

WHAT'S THIS? THAT LITTLE RED-HAIRED GIRL DROPPED HER PENCIL...

GEE... IT'S GOT TEETH MARKS ALL OVER IT...

SHE NIBBLES ON HER PENCIL...

SHE'S HUMAN!

WHAT'S THAT YOU'RE HOLDING?

IT'S A PENCIL... IT BELONGS TO THAT LITTLE RED-HAIRED GIRL... I'M GOING TO STAND HERE UNTIL SHE WALKS BY, AND THEN I'M GOING TO TELL HER HOW I FOUND IT...

I HATE TO SEE YOU GO TO ALL THAT TROUBLE, CHARLIE BROWN... WHY DON'T I JUST GIVE IT TO HER?

HEY! HERE'S YOUR STUPID PENCIL!!

WOULDN'T IT BE SOMETHING IF THAT LITTLE RED-HAIRED GIRL CAME OVER HERE AND GAVE ME A KISS?

I'D SAY, "THANK YOU! WHAT WAS THAT FOR?" AND WOULDN'T IT BE SOMETHING IF SHE SAID, "BECAUSE I'VE ALWAYS LOVED YOU!"

THEN I'D GIVE HER A BIG HUG, AND SHE'D KISS ME AGAIN! WOULDN'T THAT BE SOMETHING?

WOULDN'T IT BE SOMETHING IF IT TURNED OUT THAT FRENCH FRIES WERE GOOD FOR YOU?

YOU SHOULD GO OVER AND TALK WITH THAT LITTLE RED-HAIRED GIRL, CHARLIE BROWN

ASK HER TO EAT LUNCH WITH YOU

TELL HER YOU'D BE HAPPY JUST TO BE WITH HER FOR AN HOUR OR SO

AN HOUR? I'D SETTLE FOR AN "OR SO"!

For years, I have wanted to draw a tender, bittersweet story about Charlie Brown and the little red-haired girl where I would actually show her, but I don't think it will happen. She will probably always remain an off-stage character, for no matter how often I try, I simply can't draw her.

Several years after the *Peanuts* strip had begun running, my Dad admitted to me that he had had doubts about my being able to think of enough ideas to keep it going. This, in spite of the fact that he was always typically proud of everything I did. One day when I was eighteen, a painting contractor came into my dad's shop, and while getting his hair cut, he began to talk about his latest job which was the redecorating of one of the finest restaurants in downtown St. Paul. He said everything seemed to be relatively easy, but he was puzzled as to what he should do about the large mural that wound its way behind the bar and out into the main dining room and around the walls. He needed someone who knew something about art and oil painting to come in and "jazz it up." My dad proudly recommended me.

I knew as much about oil painting as I did cutting hair. In the correspondence course in cartooning and illustrating that I had been studying, there was a one-page article on how to paint with oils. This had been included merely to satisfy student curiosity, for the course dealt only with the commercial side of art. I actually set up an easel of sorts one day, and tried to follow the instructions that said to begin with a simple subject such as flowers, which I did. About halfway through the painting, it fell off the easel and landed face down on the carpet, and that was the last time I tried to paint anything. Now, however, I was being interviewed by the painting contractor who had returned for another haircut.

"Sure," he said, "why don't you come on down and try it. We'll give you all the stuff you need. We have brushes and paint. You'll have your primary colors. Come on down and see what you can do." Just the way he said "You'll have your primary colors" told me that he didn't know any more about this project than I did, and that I was in trouble. That night, however, I made the trip downtown and went first to a late movie to kill time before reporting to the restaurant after its midnight closing time. When I walked in, I saw a lot of activity as waiters were clearing up the evening dishes and painters were setting up scaffolding and stirring paint in big buckets. And there was the mural. Pioneers crossing America. Covered wagons, desert, brave souls facing the West all done in various shades of what could only be described as "brown."

"That's our problem," the painting contractor said. "It's just too drab. It's too dull now for the rest of the place. See what you can do to brighten it up." I looked at the mural for a few minutes trying to decide what to do. I should have looked at the door. One of the painters came over and asked if I needed any help. I told him that I thought I might begin by painting the sky a light blue, so he very cheerfully set about mixing up a shade that seemed appropriate; and with a two-inch brush that he gave me I climbed the scaffolding and started high in one corner to "brighten up the mural."

On the second night, I tried adding some streaks of red to indicate a setting sun, and amazingly enough, the painters would come by every now and then, and say, "That sure looks a lot better than that ugly brown." My progress with the two-inch brush on this huge mural was very slow. I had completed only about twenty feet by the third night, and when I walked in, I saw two regular painters filling in the sky areas around the heads of the pioneers. "I think we can handle the rest of it by ourselves," the painting contractor said to me. "Why don't you just figure out what I owe you?" I consulted with my dad about what would be a fair price. When I asked him what the minimum wage was, he told me twenty-five cents. I sent the painting contractor my bill for six dollars.

I have to admit that I don't like it when people come up to me with a three-year-old in their arms, point me out to the child and say, "Do you know who this is? This is Snoopy's father!"

An elderly couple was sitting at the table next to me in the ice arena coffee shop one morning. I noticed that she kept glancing at me, and finally she said, "I don't want to bother you, but I think I recognize you. Aren't you Snoopy's father?"

"No," I said.

"Oh, I'm sorry. You looked familiar."

"I'm Charles Schulz," I said. "And I draw Snoopy, but I'm not his father."

"VALLEY" IS THE WORD!

IF YOU WANT TO WRITE A BESTSELLER, YOU HAVE TO USE "VALLEY" IN THE TITLE...

Valley of the Beagles

I HEAR YOU'RE WRITING A DETECTIVE NOVEL

YOU SHOULD HAVE CHARACTERS IN IT WHO ARE LOOKING FOR SOMETHING VALUABLE

The Maltese Beagle

YOUR DETECTIVE ISN'T TOUGH ENOUGH

IF YOU'RE GOING TO WRITE A DETECTIVE NOVEL, YOUR DETECTIVE HAS TO BE TOUGH!

TRY TO MAKE YOUR DETECTIVE TOUGHER

He hit him again!

WHAT ARE YOU THINKING ABOUT, CHARLIE BROWN?

AM I WRONG OR DID THERE USED TO BE MORE TREES THAN THERE ARE NOW?

THEY SAY THAT WHEN THE COLONISTS FIRST CAME TO THIS COUNTRY, A SQUIRREL COULD TRAVEL TREETOP TO TREETOP FROM THE ATLANTIC TO THE MISSISSIPPI RIVER WITHOUT EVER TOUCHING THE GROUND...

BONK!
BONK!

EITHER THAT WAS A LONG TIME AGO, OR THAT WAS SOME SQUIRREL!

Why dogs are superior to cats.

They just are, and that's all there is to it!

SHORT AND TO THE POINT!

Beauty Tips

How to look younger...

Don't be born so soon.

SLEEPING AGAIN

I DON'T SEE WHY YOU NEED SO MUCH REST

I NEED PLENTY OF REST IN CASE TOMORROW IS A GREAT DAY...

IT PROBABLY WON'T BE, BUT IF IT IS, I'LL BE READY!

It was a dark and
stormy night.

Once upon a time, it was
a dark and stormy night.

HERE'S THE FIERCE JUNGLE ANIMAL PERCHED IN A TREE READY TO POUNCE ON A VICTIM WHO PASSES BELOW..

WHAT CAN YOU EXPECT FROM SOMEONE WHO GRADUATED AT THE BOTTOM OF HIS CLASS AT POUNCE SCHOOL?

For fifteen years, I have been drawing Snoopy sitting at his little portable typewriter. The other day I started a strip and completely forgot how to draw the typewriter.

This Sunday page was inspired by the memory of a strange high-command order—an order whose short life was proof of its impracticality. A few weeks after the Sunday page appeared, I was astounded to receive a letter from a retired colonel who proudly announced that he was the officer who originated the regulation. Apparently, it was an attempt to solve an epidemic of athlete's foot by forcing the men to change shoes and socks each day. He admitted to receiving much "good natured ribbing" as he traveled in the field with an inspection team. I couldn't resist telling him that we had always regarded it as one of the dumbest orders ever received. Now, I feel guilty for telling him that. It's hard to answer letters every day, however, without sometimes getting a little carried away.

Outside of drawing comic strips I think the thing that makes me the most happy is producing one of our professional ice shows at the Redwood Empire Ice Arena, which my wife and I built. It opened in 1969, and is regarded as literally the world's most beautiful ice arena. Every other year we produce a professional ice show, starring the greatest ice skaters in the world. For me to stand by the railing, watching these marvelous skaters rehearse, is happiness.

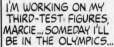
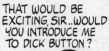

 I DON'T EVEN REMEMBER WHAT HAPPENED, SIR...

 WELL, THOSE HOCKEY PLAYERS WERE ABOUT TO GIVE ME A ROUGH TIME, AND YOU CAME RUNNING OUT TO HELP ME, MARCIE

BUT I SLIPPED AND FELL ON THE ICE, HUH?

I'LL SAY YOU DID!

 LET'S GO BACK AND SHORTEN A FEW LIFE SPANS, SIR!

LATER, MARCIE, LATER

 GUESS WHAT, SIR..WHEN I GOT HOME AND TOLD MY MOTHER ABOUT FALLING ON THE ICE, SHE CALLED THE DOCTOR...

 HE TOLD YOU TO TAKE IT EASY, HUH? WELL, THAT MAKES SENSE...CAN I GET YOU ANYTHING?

 NO, THANK YOU, SIR... I'M JUST GOING TO LIE HERE, AND TRY TO READ "PILGRIM'S PROGRESS"

 IF THE FALL ON THE ICE DIDN'T GIVE YOU A CONCUSSION, MARCIE, THAT WILL!

 I'M AFRAID I'M GOING TO BE A DISAPPOINTMENT TO YOU, MARCIE...

 I WENT OVER TO THE RINK TODAY TO GET REVENGE ON THOSE HOCKEY PLAYERS

 DID YOU PUNCH THEIR LIGHTS OUT, SIR?

I WAS GOING TO, MARCIE...

 BUT THEN THEY ASKED ME TO PLAY CENTER ON THEIR TEAM!

SCHULZ

I studied and passed the required tests to become a referee for amateur junior hockey at all levels from age five to twenty. Several friends and I became very conscientious and dedicated referees and linesmen (in spite of what the fans in the stands and certain players might say). In hockey officiating, it is required that the referee throw his left arm into the air when he is about to whistle a penalty. It becomes so ingrained that as soon as a player commits an infraction such as tripping, slashing, or elbowing an opponent, your arm immediately goes up. The blowing of the whistle then follows. After ten years of refereeing, this action has become completely automatic to me. One day I was walking through a department store and saw one shopper accidentally jostle and trip another. My left arm started to shoot into the air. Fortunately I was not carrying a whistle.

A friend of mine told me once how her young son had come home from school one day, burst through the door, hurled his jacket down on the couch, and moaned, "Mom, I feel just like Charlie Brown." He didn't have to say anything more. She knew exactly what he meant. And when someone says "She's a real Lucy!" you know who they're talking about. I suppose this is one of the things that cartoon characters can do for us—to define feelings that we can't necessarily express ourselves.

YOU LEFT YOUR CLOSET LIGHT ON ALL NIGHT...

WHO CARES?

WHO CARES?!

YOU'LL CARE WHEN YOU GET UP SOME MORNING, AND CAN'T START YOUR CLOSET

...SO THERE, SMARTY! NYAH! NYAH! NYAH!

THOSE "NYAHS" GET DOWN INTO YOUR STOMACH, AND THEN THEY JUST LAY THERE AND BURN

YOU'RE JUST AS GREEDY AS EVERYONE ELSE, CHARLIE BROWN!

DON'T COME AROUND HERE WITH YOUR LECTURES AND YOUR MOANING AND GROANING ABOUT EVERYBODY BEING GREEDY!

YOU'RE NO DIFFERENT FROM THE REST OF US!

I AM TOO!

I FEEL GUILTY ABOUT IT!!

I have always been fond of the old sayings that the previous generation laid on us. "You never miss the water 'til the well runs dry" was something I heard my mother say many times, and whenever we would return home in the evening, as we pulled into the driveway, she invariably would say, "Home again, Finnegan!" My Aunt Marian had a motto, "Never marry a trumpet player," which, of course, she eventually did. My favorite was my grandmother's: "When your children are young, they step on your toes. When they grow up, they step on your heart."

Favorite Quotations

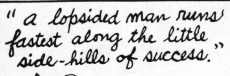

"a lopsided man runs fastest along the little side-hills of success."

WHO SAID THAT, MOSES?

NO, A MAN NAMED FRANK MOORE COLBY...

IT SOUNDS LIKE SOMETHING MOSES WOULD HAVE SAID...

ACTUALLY, IT DOESN'T SOUND AT ALL LIKE SOMETHING MOSES WOULD HAVE SAID!

HOW DO YOU KNOW? YOU NEVER TALKED TO MOSES, DID YOU?

MOSES LIKED TO SAY THINGS LIKE THAT!

IF MOSES HAD THOUGHT OF IT, MOSES WOULD HAVE SAID IT!

SCHULZ

I have underlined words and sentences in one of the Bibles that has always been my study Bible, but when I look at those words and sentences now, I can't remember why they were underlined. One day I was rereading a short story by Joanne Greenberg, and I came across a long passage that I had marked off, but as I looked at it, I couldn't remember why. Perhaps I had meant to ask her about it the next time we talked on the phone, but now I have no idea what it could be that I wanted to ask her. My Revised Standard version of the Bible is filled with markings, for I have gone through it word for word with study groups at least four times and, of course, I have used it on various occasions to begin speeches. I know that the underlined passages served some purpose, but here and there are verses that have no special meaning to me. It is almost as if a friend had secretly opened the book and made some markings just to tease me. What was the spirit trying to say to me then that I no longer need to hear? Or, what was I listening for then that I no longer care about?

For the past three years, we have hosted a professional senior tennis tournament at the Ice Arena in Santa Rosa with such stars as Billie Jean King, Rosie Casals, and Virginia Wade. The tournament is called The Women's Tennis Classic, and the winner's trophy the Snoopy Cup. This year Kerry Ried flew in from Hilton Head to join the group, and on her first night in California, she phoned home to talk to her husband and two little girls. The three-year-old said, "Good luck, Mommy. . . . Bring home the Smurf Cup."

In 1974 I was invited by Mr. Ed Wilson, president of that year's Tournament of Roses Parade in Pasadena, to be the grand marshal. On the day before the parade, we were guests at a very large luncheon. A band was playing as we entered the hall, and the conductor asked me what my favorite number was. I must have been overwhelmed by the grandness of the occasion, because not understanding the question, I said, "two."

WHAT ARE YOU WATCHING? — THE "ROSE PARADE" FROM PASADENA

THEY HAVE SOME OF THE MOST BEAUTIFUL FLOATS THIS YEAR I'VE EVER SEEN

HAS THE GRAND MARSHAL GONE BY YET? — YEAH, YOU MISSED HIM...

BUT HE WASN'T ANYONE YOU EVER HEARD OF!

I KNOW THE ANSWER!

THE ANSWER LIES WITHIN THE HEART OF ALL MANKIND!

THE ANSWER WAS "TWELVE," SIR

I THINK I'M IN THE WRONG BUILDING!

MY DOG NEVER OBEYS COMMANDS..OTHER DOGS WILL "SIT" OR "HEEL"

MY DOG HAS ONLY OBEYED ONE COMMAND IN HIS LIFE...

I ONCE TOLD HIM TO "STAY," AND HE NEVER WENT HOME!

HOW EMBARRASSING! I'VE ALWAYS THOUGHT IT WAS AN INVITATION...

MA'AM?

NO, I DON'T HAVE ANY IDEA

I'M AFRAID MY BRAIN HAS LEFT FOR THE DAY

WOULD YOU CARE TO LEAVE A MESSAGE WITH THE ANSWERING SERVICE?

YOU LOOK LIKE YOU'RE SINKING, SIR...

I AM, MARCIE

I'M DROWNING IN A SEA OF UNANSWERED QUESTIONS...

NOW, I SUDDENLY SURFACE! I SPLASH FRANTICALLY... "HELP!" I CRY..."SAVE ME!"

NOW, I SINK FOR THE SECOND TIME...QUESTIONS POUR OVER MY HEAD..."WHO WAS VOLTAIRE?" "WHO WAS CATO THE ELDER?"

NOW, I COME UP FOR THE LAST TIME... SPUTTERING HALF-ANSWERS..SPITTING OUT VERBS, INFINITIVES, COMMAS...

I SINK BENEATH THE SURFACE.. I'M GONE, MARCIE... I'M GONE...

MARK THE SPOT WHERE YOU LAST SAW ME..MARK THE SPOT WHERE I DROWNED IN A SEA OF "D MINUSES" AND "INCOMPLETES"

ANOTHER SCHOLAR CAUGHT IN THE UNDERTOW, MA'AM

Some time in the early part of 1980, I received a phone call from attorney Stephen Trattner of Washington, D.C. He told me that he represented Skippy, Inc., the "successor-in-interest and owner of federal and common law trademarks in the term SKIPPY, emanating from the *Skippy* cartoon and comic strip created by Percy L. Crosby in 1923." His client was suing CPC International, Inc., for illegal use of the name "Skippy" on their peanut butter product. He asked if I would be willing to be an "expert witness" in the trial. At first, I was very doubtful of his chances, even though I was certain in my own mind that the theft of the famous cartoon name was obvious. He explained several points of law, however, that easily persuaded me at least to submit to a deposition, and he added that Mr. Milton Caniff, famous creator of *Terry and the Pirates* and *Steve Canyon*, had also agreed to be an expert witness.

The deposition was interesting because I felt able to counter any suggestions that the label on the peanut butter jars did not really reflect Percy Crosby's style. I was able, I felt, to explain how a simple drawing of a board fence with heavy brush stroke lettering was easily identified and had been as much a part of *Skippy* as Snoopy's doghouse is in *Peanuts*, and that these symbols, when used over and over, actually help to promote creativity and produce ideas. At one point in the questioning, I was asked by attorney Joanne Alper, "Is it your testimony that Crosby had exclusive rights to the use of a fence in a comic strip?"

"No," I replied. "If I were to create a label, knowing that I could not use the *Skippy* character itself, and wanted to use the name 'Skippy' and pick an element that people would recognize and know that this was related to the *Skippy* comic strip, I would have picked one of two things. I would have drawn the homemade go-cart that they always had and lettered 'Skippy' on the side, knowing that people would immediately say that was Skippy's go-cart; or, I would have used one of his typical wooden fences and used his style of lettering."

What I was trying to get into the record was my opinion of how an advertising agency might borrow some valuable elements from a successful cartoon that would be recognized by everyone without actually using the main character. I also was anxious to further Stephen Trattner's contention that the use of the fence and the lettering was just as much a theft as the use of Skippy's face would have been. I thought I had made some good points, and was ready for the trial, wondering, too, what sort of de-position Milt had given. Milt Caniff is one of the most remarkable men in the history of cartooning. I have seen him in meetings where he has sat, appearing almost not to be listening at all, but then rising to make a point that was swift, sure, and sensible. Stephen Trattner met Jeannie, Milt, and me at Dulles Airport in August, and on our way into the city, we discussed the issues of the trial, and Milt remarked, "We've got to show them that we've come to play hard ball!" I was confident that I had a good partner.

That evening, we attended a dinner at a beautiful country club where we met various relatives of Joan Crosby Tibbetts and the attorneys. Confidence was everywhere as we all agreed to the righteousness of our cause; Milt and I especially, feeling that we were doing something for the memory of Percy Crosby and for the comic industry itself. We were about to right a terrible wrong. My wife, Jeannie, recalled that at one point, attorney Trattner asked her, "What do you think is the most important point I should try to get across?" She was caught up in the enthusiasm of the guests at the dinner and told Stephen that he should try to bring out the tragic history of Percy Crosby's incarceration in the mental ward of King's Park Veterans' Hospital on Long Island for sixteen years, where he eventually died. He should try to convince the judge that Crosby's inability to communicate from his imprisonment caused the time-delay in bringing any action to stop the use of the *Skippy* name. He should try to convince the judge that justice should be done, even though, legally, the statute of limitations had apparently expired. Much to her embarrassment, the next day at the trial, the judge wouldn't even listen to this story, and said, "We know all this. We don't have to listen to this. Get on with the case." Jeannie thought to herself, "I should have kept my mouth shut."

Stephen Trattner was late meeting us for breakfast the next day, the trial day, because he said he had been making some last minute additions to his opening statement. We left our hotel to walk the short distance to the courthouse. After walking three blocks, Stephen said, "I think we're going in the wrong direction!" This statement, revealing his obvious ner-vousness, amused me and later prompted a Snoopy cartoon.

The courtroom had a lot more people in it than we had expected, and Judge Oren Lewis apparently was as surprised, for his first words were,

"What are all these people doing here? I hope they're not all witnesses!" Judge Lewis, I was told, was frequently referred to as "Roarin' Oren," and his actions could terrify attorneys. We could see this immediately as Joanne Alper, representing CPC International, Inc., began her opening statements. It did my heart good to see her suffer the remarks of the judge, for I considered her behavior to Stephen during my deposition as unnecessarily rude. Judge Lewis continually interrupted both attorneys, finally demanding that "he didn't have to hear all of this," that the case really was "cut and dried," and "let's hear a witness. Get on with the case." Milt Caniff was called to the stand, asked to identify himself, etc., and then, without being given the opportunity to testify to anything, was dismissed. It was disappointing and actually degrading. It taught me, however, that as I was called to take the oath, not to say anything beyond "Yes, sir" and "No, sir." I had one very brief skirmish with the opposing attorney as she tried to have me admit that "Skippy" was not necessarily a unique or original name. Shortly thereafter, we were dismissed, and found ourselves out in the hall grumbling about the ridiculousness of the whole episode, and questioning the tenure of federal court justices.

Joan Crosby Tibbetts thanked us for coming all the way across the country to try to help, especially at our own expense. I told her that if she really wanted to thank me in a material way, I would love to have an original *Skippy* Sunday page, and she agreed to send me one.

The following April, I received a letter from Attorney Stephen Trattner, informing me that Judge Lewis ruled against them, but that he was filing an appeal. I have heard nothing more from him, although we do exchange Christmas cards, and I have never received the original *Skippy* Sunday page.

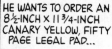

HERE'S THE WORLD FAMOUS ATTORNEY ON HIS WAY TO THE COURTHOUSE...

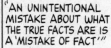

"AN UNINTENTIONAL MISTAKE ABOUT WHAT THE TRUE FACTS ARE IS A 'MISTAKE OF FACT'"

THEN I WAS RIGHT..

LUNCH IS AT ONE-THIRTY!

HERE'S THE WORLD FAMOUS ATTORNEY ON HIS WAY TO THE COURTHOUSE...

THIS IS A MAXIM OF JURISPRUDENCE..."A THING CONTINUES TO EXIST AS LONG AS IS USUAL WITH THINGS OF THIS NATURE"

DID YOU UNDERSTAND THAT?

I DIDN'T EVEN UNDERSTAND THE LUNCH MENU!

HERE'S THE WORLD FAMOUS LAWYER ON HIS WAY TO THE COURTHOUSE

WHEN LAWYERS SAY, "SINE MORA," THEY MEAN, "WITHOUT DELAY"

LAWYERS SAY A LOT OF THINGS

THE COURT WILL NOT AID THOSE WHO HAVE COMMITTED ILLEGAL ACTS IN A MATTER...

..AND THEN ASK THE COURT'S HELP TO RECOVER FOR ANY INJURY THEY MAY HAVE SUFFERED AS A RESULT THEREOF!

RATS!

I think one of the worst traits that a person can have is to possess sensitive areas that make others uncomfortable. No one can relax around someone who is so sensitive about his religious, political, or other beliefs that they have to watch everything they say.

There must be different kinds of loneliness, or at least different degrees of loneliness, but the most terrifying loneliness is not experienced by everyone and can be understood by only a few. I compare the panic in this kind of loneliness to the dog we see running frantically down the road pursuing the family car. He is not really being left behind, for the family knows it is to return, but for that moment in his limited understanding, he is being left alone forever, and he has to run and run to survive. It is no wonder that we make terrible choices in our lives to avoid loneliness.

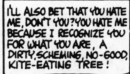

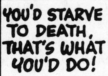

I always enjoy drawing the episodes where Marcie and Peppermint Patty are attending a "Tiny Tots" concert. They always complain that each time they go, the orchestra plays "Peter and the Wolf" and I am certain that there is a lot of truth in this.

Some time in the sixties, I was approached by the conductor of the San Francisco Youth Symphony to perform "Peter and the Wolf" with them. I warned him that I know nothing about music, and even though I would be reading the narrative, I probably would have no idea when to speak and when to remain silent. He assured me that there would be no problem because he would be right next to me on the stage and could easily cue me. He even offered to go over the score with me, but soon found this to be useless because I could not read music. He left me with a recording of the work as recited by Peter Ustinov. This saved me, for I listened to the recording at least fifty times, and made my own crude notes such as "the violins go zip, zip, zip," and on the day of the performance made only one very slight miscue.

All in all it was a great triumph for one who still sits in awe at symphony concerts watching musicians perform. I am not sure, however, that all of the music played at these "Tiny Tots" concerts is as inspiring to these little ones as the committees who arrange the programs would like to think they are. I saw a concert on television one day, and when the camera panned through the audience, each child's face seemed to indicate that he or she just might prefer to be somewhere else.

In 1978, I was informed by Monsieur Robert LePalme of the International Pavilion of Humor of Montreal, Canada, that I had been selected as International Cartoonist of the Year. He invited me to attend the judging of their yearly cartoon contest, and to be the honorary chairman of the judging committee. On the first evening, my wife, Jeannie, Lee Mendelson, our TV producer, and I were guests at what was to us a very nice affair. As vichyssoise was being served, Lee spoke loudly to me across the table: "Eat your soup, Sparky, before it gets cold."

"Sir," said the very proper man seated next to Lee, "it is supposed to be cold!"

Monsieur LePalme is a delightful man, short in stature, but very tall in humor and dignity. He had been very anxious for us to enjoy ourselves while we were in Montreal, but for some reason, that first dinner was to him a great disappointment. Things just were not up to his standard. Therefore, he wanted everything on the next evening to be perfect. I asked him how we should dress for this dinner.

"Should we wear ties?"

"Yes, we should wear ties."

"Why?" I asked. "Who is going to be there?"

"We shall dress for ourselves," said LePalme.

When we got to the restaurant, LePalme told the owner that he was placing us in his hands, and to serve us whatever he thought we might like. The dinner, of course, was excellent, and the wines were as special as LePalme hoped they would be, although I certainly couldn't tell, being as ignorant of wine as it is possible to be. Along about eleven o'clock, I noticed that I had accumulated a row of glasses in front of me that was quite impressive; a water glass, two red wines (untouched), two white wines (only slightly touched), and a Seven-Up. Robert LePalme looked at this row of glasses, leaned over to me and asked, "May I say something to you?"

"Yes, Robert. What is it?"

"I do not wish to offend."

"That's all right, Robert, a little offending never hurt anybody."

"You," he said, "are the most simple man I have ever met."

SUPPERTIME!

SUPPERTIME!
SUPPERTIME!

OH, IT'S SUPPERTIME! IT'S SUPPERTIME!!!

YAHOO! IT'S SUPPERTIME!

SUPPERTIME! SUPPERTIME! SUPPERTIME!
GOOD OL' SUP, SUP, SUP, SUPPERTIME!

SUPPERTIME!

I MUST ADMIT HE'S A VERY
SATISFYING PERSON TO COOK FOR

A high school student wrote to me once as part of a class project, asking me if I would name my three heroes. I answered, "General Eisenhower, Billie Jean King, and Sam Snead." I have often wondered what the teacher's reaction was.

OLGA KORBUT HAS BEEN BUGGING ME FOR LESSONS!

MARCIE, HELP ME PICK OUT A LIBRARY BOOK

MAYBE SOMETHING ABOUT PATTY BERG..SHE'S ONE OF MY IDOLS...

MOSES WARNED US ABOUT WORSHIPPING IDOLS, SIR...

MOSES NEVER SAW PATTY BERG HIT A SEVEN-IRON!

WHAT ARE YOU DOING?

I'M TRYING TO COME UP WITH SOME KIND OF ITEM I CAN SELL DURING THE BICENTENNIAL, AND MAKE A MILLION DOLLARS...

HOW DOES THIS LOOK? IT'S A DRAWING OF GEORGE WASHINGTON, BETSY ROSS, HARRY TRUMAN AND BILLIE JEAN KING PLAYING MIXED DOUBLES!

THAT'S PATRIOTIC, ISN'T IT?

HARRY AND BILLIE JEAN WOULD TAKE 'EM IN STRAIGHT SETS!

THERE'S THE HOUSE WHERE THAT LITTLE RED-HAIRED GIRL LIVES...

MAYBE SHE'LL SEE ME, AND COME RUSHING OUT TO THANK ME FOR THE CHRISTMAS CARD I SENT HER...MAYBE SHE'LL EVEN GIVE ME A HUG...

MAYBE BILLIE JEAN KING WILL CALL ME TONIGHT, AND INVITE ME OUT TO DINNER

When you're a professional, creativity should not require certain moods, although I will admit that moods of despair or even loneliness seem, strangely enough, to produce good humor. If you are a person who looks at the funny side of things, then sometimes when you are the lowest, when everything seems totally hopeless, you will come up with some of your best ideas.

Happiness does not create humor. There's nothing funny about being happy. Sadness creates humor. Krazy Kat getting hit on the head by a brick from Ignatz Mouse is funny. All the sad things that happen to Charlie Chaplin are funny. It's funny because it's not happening to us.

I HEARD SOMEONE ON TV SAY THAT THE WORLD IS GETTING WORSE EVERY DAY

THAT'S RIDICULOUS!

HOW COULD THE WORLD BE GETTING WORSE WITH ME IN IT? EVER SINCE I WAS BORN THE WORLD HAS SHOWN A DISTINCT IMPROVEMENT!

I MAKE THE WORLD BETTER! I'M A POSITIVE FORCE!

SMILE!

SEE? WITH ME AROUND, EVERYONE IS A LOT HAPPIER!

No. 1
CRAB

SLAM!

BOY, DO I FEEL CRABBY!

MAYBE I CAN BE OF HELP

WHY DON'T YOU JUST TAKE MY PLACE HERE IN FRONT OF THE TV WHILE I GO AND FIX YOU A NICE SNACK?

SOMETIMES WE ALL NEED A LITTLE PAMPERING TO HELP US FEEL BETTER...

SEE? I CAME RIGHT BACK! HERE'S A NICE SANDWICH FOR YOU, SOME CHOCOLATE CHIP COOKIES AND A COLD GLASS OF MILK...

NOW, IS THERE ANYTHING ELSE I CAN GET YOU?

IS THERE ANYTHING I HAVEN'T THOUGHT OF?

YES, THERE'S ONE THING THAT YOU HAVEN'T THOUGHT OF.....

I DON'T WANNA FEEL BETTER!!

On July 1, 1981, I awakened with a strange tight feeling in my chest. At first, I attributed it to having slept crooked during the night. As I dressed and then went into the kitchen, the feeling persisted, and I mentioned it to Jeannie, and a house guest. I almost turned around when driving to the studio, for the strange tightness wouldn't go away. Perhaps I'd be better off returning home. A few very deep breaths seemed to help, however, and I continued to drive. I tried to begin work, but as I sat at the drawing board, the tightness began again.

If it had not been that a very close friend of ours, Raul Diez, had gone into the hospital three days before with blood clots that traveled to his lungs, I believe I would have gone home and simply sat by the pool for the rest of the morning, dismissing the symptoms as being something that would soon pass. But, maybe what had happened to Raul was now happening to me. Dr. Lundborg's nurse said I should come in immediately, and a few quick tests convinced him to call a cardiologist who ordered me directly to the hospital. In the midst of all the tests that took up the rest of the morning, I drew a cartoon of myself lying in bed saying, "Hey, Raul, what are we doing in here?" Jeannie took it down the hall to Raul who, of course, was stunned to discover that now both of us were in trouble.

Eventually Raul struggled through several frightening crises and returned to good health. I had a two-month period where I had to decide if the four practically closed arteries that were discovered warranted by-pass surgery. It is always fascinating to look back and see what little incidents sometimes cause us to make big decisions. Jeannie and I visited Dr. Ted Folkerth, the heart surgeon, to find out once and for all just what the surgery would be like. He offered to let me see some films, but I quickly declined. My greatest fear was the knowledge that they sawed your chest open. Ted assured me that this was very simple and relatively painless. During the casual questioning and conversation, I drew out of him the story of his returning to Vietnam for a second tour of duty to learn more of surgery. It was then that I thought, "If anyone goes back to Vietnam a second time to become a better surgeon, certainly I can trust him!" Many months later, I reminded him of this. "I don't remember saying that at all," he remarked.

On the fourth night after the surgery, I lay in bed staring at the blank wall across the room. Jeannie was sitting quietly next to the bed reading the paper. When I was first admitted to the hospital, one of the nurses placed a large felt-tip pen on a cabinet and said, "Before you leave here, we want you to draw something on the wall." I am not one who goes around drawing pictures on the wall, but I felt I had to fulfill this request. It was now almost ten-thirty at night, and like all cartoon ideas, it suddenly came to me. I climbed carefully out of bed, picked up the pen and began to draw a series of five Snoopys, showing him struggling with an inhalator to make the three balls rise to the top and remain there for a moment. All patients could identify with this frustrating exercise, devised to keep the lungs clear and get them back to good working order. The last panel showed him collapsing with exhaustion and triumph.

The triumph, of course, belonged also to Jeannie and me. It was a difficult decision just to have the surgery, but now here I was standing at the wall, drawing again, exhilarated with the feeling that I had gone through something I had not been sure I was brave enough to attempt, and that maybe, somehow, drawing cartoons really was what I was meant to do.

Panel 1: I KEPT MY PROMISE, DIDN'T I? I DIDN'T PULL THE BALL AWAY

Panel 2: NO, YOU'RE RIGHT... YOU DIDN'T

Panel 3: BUT I MISSED THE BALL, AND KICKED YOUR HAND... I DON'T KNOW WHAT TO SAY.. IS THERE ANYTHING I CAN DO?

Panel 4: NEXT TIME YOU GO TO THE HOSPITAL, STAY THERE!

Panel 1: YOU A DOCTOR! HA! THAT'S A BIG LAUGH!

Panel 2: YOU COULD NEVER BE A DOCTOR! YOU KNOW WHY?

Panel 3: BECAUSE YOU DON'T LOVE MANKIND, THAT'S WHY!

Panel 4: I LOVE MANKIND... IT'S PEOPLE I CAN'T STAND!!

Panel 1: THIS IS THE LAST DAY OF THE YEAR

Panel 2: ALL IN ALL, IT WASN'T SO BAD

Panel 3: YOU KNOW WHAT I LIKED ABOUT THIS YEAR?

Panel 4: I'M STILL IN IT!

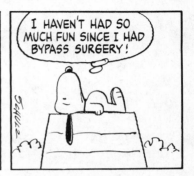

I don't believe that animation is superior as a medium to the comic strip any more than the novel is superior to the short story, or the stage to the movie screen. There are expanses, however, that can be attained through animation, where the simple, tiny squares of the comic strip are limiting. Our first animated half-hour specials were a direct outgrowth of the newspaper comic strips with the addition of slightly more detailed backgrounds and music being really the only difference. As we progressed to large-screen movies and more television shows, I began to grow impatient with what we were doing. I wanted to develop more emotion in our scenes and our stories.

The last movie, "Bon Voyage, Charlie Brown," showed the kids in France as exchange students. The ending was purposely open-ended in case we decided to do something else with them in Europe before their final return home. The last scene showed them bidding their recent friends good-bye, and then piling into the little French car with Snoopy driving, and heading up the road to Paris and the airport. I kept thinking how interesting it might be if they should get lost on this little trip and somehow end up at Omaha Beach and the scenes of the famous D-Day invasion of World War II. I even thought that they might pass through Belgium and we could show some landscapes affected by World War I, and how emotional it could be if one of the characters somehow could be made to recite the immortal poem "In Flanders Field."

None of this fit together in a reasonable way, however, until one night soon after my heart surgery when I was lying awake at about three o'clock in the morning. After your chest has been sawed in half, sleeping on one's back is a definite requirement for at least a few weeks, and of course sleep does not always come as easily in this restricted position. While lying there staring into the dark, I began to think some more about the story line that I wanted for this show. I knew if I could get just one phrase I could tie the whole thing together. All of a sudden the line, "What have we learned, Charlie Brown?" came to me. This helped everything else fall into place, and as soon as I got home I called Bill Melendez, the animator, and we agreed that we had something really new and different to add to television cartoon programming. The Peabody Award we received for "What Have We Learned, Charlie Brown?" was a very gratifying response to the program, plus many wonderful letters from appreciative young viewers who said that they now understood a little better what happened on June 6, 1944. We labeled this show with the subtitle "A Tribute," because that was exactly what we wanted it to be; no more and certainly no less. It proved also that the characters of Charlie Brown, Linus, Snoopy, and the others were close enough to being real to handle delicately a subject that other animated characters would destroy.

 HOLD ON TO YOUR LEG WARMERS, MARCIE! HAVE I GOT NEWS! I'VE BEEN DEPRESSED ABOUT FAILING ALL MY CLASSES, RIGHT?

 SO THE SCHOOL PSYCHOLOGIST ADVISED MY DAD TO TAKE ME WITH HIM TO EUROPE THIS SUMMER! HOW ABOUT THAT?

 YEARS AGO THERE USED TO BE A RADIO PROGRAM CALLED "IT PAYS TO BE IGNORANT"

 JEALOUSY DOES NOT BECOME YOU, MARCIE!

 LOOK, CHARLES... I GOT A POST CARD FROM PATTY.. SHE'S IN PARIS...

 Dear Marcie, The trip over was fun. We have a nice place to stay.

 I'm already doing pretty good with the language.

 BONJOUR, KID!

 Dear Chuck, Well, your ol' friend Patty is here in Paris.

 Show Snoopy this picture of me drinking root beer in a sidewalk cafe.

 I REMEMBER THAT PLACE.. I WAS THERE IN 1918!

 Dear Chuck, Here is a photo of me in front of a World War II pillbox near Honfleur.

 I am learning a lot and my French is getting better and better.

 AU REVOIR, KID!

 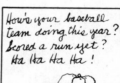 

There is a bookstore in Santa Rosa just a few blocks from the Ice Arena where I spend a lot of time, and two more blocks from the studio. I'm a virtual bookaholic—I find it very difficult to go home at night without stopping by and seeing what new things are in. There's an ice cream store right next to the bookstore, and on the front of the bookstore there's a little sign that says "No ice cream allowed," which is understandable. One day I went into the ice cream store and I said to the guy behind the counter, "It is all right if you bring books in here?" I don't think he had any idea what I was talking about.

I really never make appearances in classrooms because I don't feel that I am especially good at that sort of thing. And I've always had the theory that cartoonists shouldn't venture out in public too much, talking. They should stay at home and sit behind the drawing board, drawing. But recently I relented as a special favor to a close friend and found myself in front of a kindergarten class. The teacher asked me to draw a Snoopy on the chalkboard. Now all my life I've always wanted to draw on a big chalkboard. When I was a little kid in school you never got to draw on the chalkboard—you had to stand up there in front of the class and make a fool out of yourself doing geometry on it, but you never got to draw. This was my chance to draw on a beautiful big green chalkboard. So I drew one of my great Snoopys, turned around and said, "Well, what do you think?" One little kid stood up and said, "Can't you draw a better one than that?"

YES, MA'AM, I'M READY...

FOR MY NATURE REPORT TODAY, I AM BRINGING YOU AN EXCLUSIVE!

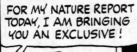

ROCK SNAKES!!

WHAT, YOU MAY ASK, IS A ROCK SNAKE? THAT IS A GOOD QUESTION! A ROCK SNAKE IS A SNAKE THAT SNEAKS UP BEHIND YOU, AND THROWS A ROCK AT YOU!

NOW, HERE IS MY EXCLUSIVE...IT USED TO BE THOUGHT THAT ROCK SNAKES WERE DANGEROUS, BUT MY AUTHORITY SAYS THIS IS NOT SO...

A ROCK SNAKE CANNOT THROW VERY HIGH, YOU SEE, SO THEREFORE, ALL HE CAN DO IS HIT YOU ON THE BACK OF THE LEG...SO SAYS MY AUTHORITY!

MA'AM?

LINUS VAN PELT.... YES, MA'AM..

SHE SAID SHE REMEMBERS YOU FROM WHEN YOU WERE IN HER CLASS!

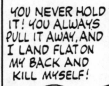

Why does Lucy pull away the football every time Charlie Brown comes running up to kick it, and why does he let himself be fooled so often? Obviously, she has a mean streak in her and he has a trusting personality, but readers can certainly see other bits of symbolism there if they wish.

Of course, it all started with memories of our own games, when we were about that age. It was absolutely impossible for anyone to hold the ball on the kickoff. The urge to pull it away was irresistible. Maybe this is what

drives Lucy. She really can't help herself. Perhaps she is also annoyed that it is all too easy. Charlie Brown isn't that much of a challenge.

To be consistent, however, we have to let her triumph, for all the loves in the strip are unrequited; all the baseball games are lost; all the test grades are D-minuses; the Great Pumpkin never comes and the football is always pulled away.

In 1965, the class I graduated with was planning its twenty-fifth reunion. I was on the list of people they didn't know what had happened to.